MAYER SMITH

Behind Closed Doors with My Billionaire Boss

Copyright © 2025 by Mayer Smith

All rights reserved. No part of this publication may be reproduced, stored or transmitted in any form or by any means, electronic, mechanical, photocopying, recording, scanning, or otherwise without written permission from the publisher. It is illegal to copy this book, post it to a website, or distribute it by any other means without permission.

This novel is entirely a work of fiction. The names, characters and incidents portrayed in it are the work of the author's imagination. Any resemblance to actual persons, living or dead, events or localities is entirely coincidental.

Mayer Smith asserts the moral right to be identified as the author of this work.

Mayer Smith has no responsibility for the persistence or accuracy of URLs for external or third-party Internet Websites referred to in this publication and does not guarantee that any content on such Websites is, or will remain, accurate or appropriate.

Designations used by companies to distinguish their products are often claimed as trademarks. All brand names and product names used in this book and on its cover are trade names, service marks, trademarks and registered trademarks of their respective owners. The publishers and the book are not associated with any product or vendor mentioned in this book. None of the companies referenced within the book have endorsed the book.

First edition

This book was professionally typeset on Reedsy. Find out more at reedsy.com

Contents

1	Hidden Billionaire	1
2	A Chance Encounter	7
3	Behind the Mask	14
4	The Unseen Connection	21
5	Connection	28
6	Love	35
7	Another Life	42
8	Watchers	49
9	Reality	56
10	The Cost	63
11	Divided	70
12	Test of Fate	76
13	Universes	82
14	Love in the Void	89
15	Rebond	95

One

Hidden Billionaire

The office was filled with the usual hum of busy employees typing away, phones ringing, and the occasional low murmur of whispered conversations. It was the perfect setting for someone like Julian Sterling—someone who wanted to remain invisible, unnoticed amidst the bustle of a company where no one knew his true identity. He sat in the back corner of the room, hidden in the shadows, his face partly obscured by a pair of sleek, dark sunglasses.

No one would recognize him. Not here. Not now.

Julian had always been a man who thrived on secrecy. The anonymity was his armor, a way to shield himself from the judgments that would inevitably come if anyone discovered the truth about who he really was. In the world he inhabited, fame was as much a curse as a blessing. His wealth, power, and status would make him the subject of countless eyes, whispers, and assumptions. That's why he carefully guarded his true identity, walking through the world as a man without a past, and most certainly without a future that was mapped out by others.

Today, he was no different than the low-level executives in the room, who worked tirelessly to please their bosses. Julian wore the same drab gray suit as the others, his tie knotted loosely, his hair tousled as if he had just rolled out of bed. He didn't need the polished image of the billionaire everyone thought he was. He needed to be one of them—anonymous, just another face in the crowd.

The only problem was that someone had noticed him.

Her name was Emily Hart, and she was far from ordinary.

Emily was the company's new HR director, brought in to whip the department into shape and help manage the growing issues surrounding employee engagement. She was sharp, confident, and had a way of seeing through people that unnerved some of her colleagues. What no one knew about Emily was that she had a gift—a rare ability to read between the lines, to spot the cracks in a person's façade, to sense when something wasn't quite right.

As she walked through the office, clipboard in hand, she felt a pull toward Julian. It wasn't just his reserved demeanor that caught her attention; it was the aura around him. He wasn't like the others in the room. There was an underlying tension to him, something that didn't belong in a place like this—a deep, guarded energy that made Emily pause and look twice.

He didn't belong here. He didn't belong anywhere.

The first time they crossed paths, Emily had dismissed it as coincidence. But there was something magnetic about Julian, an enigma she couldn't ignore. He was always there, lurking in the corners of meetings, slipping in and out of the building at odd hours, never saying much, always blending in. It was as if he was hiding, playing the part of a man trying to disappear.

But Emily wasn't so easily fooled.

She had seen men like him before—men who wore their wealth as armor, who built walls around themselves so high that no one could get close enough to see their true face. There was something almost tragic about it. The constant running, the desperate need to be invisible, to escape the expectations of a world that constantly watched.

Curiosity gnawed at Emily. She needed to know more.

Her first opportunity came on a Friday afternoon. The office was quieter than usual, with many of the employees taking an early exit to start their weekend. Julian, however, was still at his desk, pretending to be just another cog in the machine, his fingers poised over his keyboard as though he was hard at work. But Emily knew better. She could tell when someone was faking it.

Taking a deep breath, she approached his desk with a calm,

confident stride. As she neared, she noticed his head snap up slightly, his eyes hidden behind the dark lenses of his sunglasses, a slight shift in his posture. He was aware of her approach, but he didn't look at her directly, keeping his focus trained on the screen in front of him.

"Mr. Sterling," she said, her voice smooth and authoritative. "Can I have a moment of your time?"

Julian's fingers paused midair, his expression unreadable as he slowly turned his head toward her. Despite the sunglasses, she could feel the weight of his gaze. He wasn't fazed by her presence, but there was a subtle tension in the air, as if he was carefully calculating how to respond.

"Of course, Ms. Hart," he replied, his voice deep, with a hint of detachment. "What can I do for you?"

Emily wasn't fooled. She had no doubt he knew exactly who she was and what she wanted. But it wasn't what she wanted to discuss that mattered—it was what he wasn't saying, the way he held himself back, the way he tried to act like he was just another employee.

"I wanted to go over a few things regarding the employee engagement program," Emily continued, leaning slightly against the edge of his desk. She let her eyes linger on him for a moment, studying his face for any sign of vulnerability. "We're looking to make some changes, and I thought it would be good to get your feedback."

Julian gave a curt nod, his lips tight as if he was trying to suppress any emotion. "I'm happy to provide input, Ms. Hart. Please, go ahead."

The conversation began, but Emily wasn't focused on the project anymore. She was watching him, analyzing his every move, his every word. He was a man used to being in control, but there was something about him that felt out of place here. The way he spoke—precise, but distant. The way he sat—always a little too composed, as if he were afraid of showing too much of himself.

Something about Julian Sterling didn't sit right with her.

As they continued talking about the engagement program, Emily found herself distracted by the thought of him—this man who was hiding something. And she couldn't help but wonder: what was he running from? What secret was he keeping locked away behind those dark glasses and impenetrable walls?

She decided then and there that she would find out. She wasn't going to let this go.

The meeting ended shortly after, with Julian excusing himself with his usual quiet grace. As he stood and walked past her, their eyes met briefly, and Emily saw something flicker in his expression—was it guilt? Regret? Or maybe, just maybe, it was fear.

Emily watched him disappear into the elevator, a sense of foreboding creeping up her spine. There was something more to Julian Sterling, something that was just beneath the surface. And she would uncover it, no matter what it took.

What she didn't know, however, was that Julian was already aware of her scrutiny. He had known the moment she walked into the room that she would be different. The moment she looked at him with those perceptive eyes, he had felt the weight of her gaze, and it unnerved him more than he cared to admit.

She was too smart. Too curious.

And that was dangerous.

Julian knew he had to be careful. Emily Hart wasn't going to let him slip through the cracks like everyone else. She was a woman who would find the truth—and the truth about him was something he could never let her see. Not now. Not ever.

As he watched the elevator doors close behind him, Julian made a silent vow to himself. He had to keep his secret safe. He had to keep her out.

But as the days wore on, he would soon find that it was easier to hide from the world than it was to hide from Emily Hart.

Two

A Chance Encounter

The following Monday was like every other day at Sterling Enterprises. The office was buzzing with activity, employees rushing around with files, phones ringing incessantly, and the hum of typing keyboards filling the air. But for Emily Hart, today felt different. Something had shifted after her brief encounter with Julian Sterling, the mysterious man who had been a puzzle she couldn't quite piece together. The more she thought about him, the more questions kept circling her mind. Why was he hiding behind that carefully constructed disguise? What was he running from?

The hallway outside the HR department was quiet when she arrived at work, and as Emily settled into her office, she couldn't help but glance toward the windows that overlooked the city. The weather was dreary—grey clouds hanging low in the sky, the rain gently tapping against the glass. It felt like the world was preparing for something that was about to unfold, something that she wasn't yet fully aware of.

She had always prided herself on being able to read people, to see through their facades and understand their true nature. But Julian Sterling... he was different. The moment they spoke, she knew there was more beneath the surface. There was an intensity about him, a coldness that contrasted with the warmth she saw flicker in his eyes every now and then. A part of her couldn't let go of the need to understand what made him tick.

As Emily sat at her desk, reviewing employee engagement reports, the door to her office creaked open, and her assistant, Sarah, stepped inside. She was a young woman, eager and friendly, her face always wearing a smile.

"Ms. Hart, there's a man here to see you," Sarah said, her voice polite yet uncertain. "He says it's urgent."

Emily raised an eyebrow. "A man? Who is he?"

Sarah hesitated for a moment. "He didn't say, but... well, he looks important."

"Important?" Emily repeated, her curiosity piqued. "Send him in."

Moments later, the door swung open, and a tall figure stepped into her office. Julian Sterling. But this time, there was something different in the way he carried himself. He wasn't wearing the dark sunglasses or the carefully curated disguise.

Instead, he wore a black suit, sharp and tailored, his hair combed back neatly. His expression was unreadable as he walked toward her desk, his presence commanding, yet oddly distant.

"Ms. Hart," he said, his deep voice filling the room. "I hope I'm not interrupting anything."

Emily stood up, trying not to let the surprise show on her face. The last thing she expected was for Julian to seek her out, especially after their tense conversation on Friday. He had been cold, guarded, yet there was something in his eyes that told her he hadn't forgotten their encounter.

"No, not at all. Please, take a seat," Emily said, motioning to the chair across from her.

Julian didn't sit immediately. Instead, he walked to the window, his gaze briefly lingering on the rain outside before he turned back to her. "I needed to speak with you," he said, his tone grave. "It's about the employee engagement program."

Emily felt a flicker of disappointment. Of course, it was about work. She had hoped that his sudden appearance might signal something more. But at the same time, she reminded herself, this was his world—professional, polished, and full of walls.

"I'm listening," she said, folding her hands on the desk.

Julian walked toward the chair and finally sat down, though he didn't fully relax. There was a tension in his posture, as if he was carefully calculating each word before it left his mouth.

"I've been thinking about what you said on Friday," he began. "You mentioned that some changes were needed to improve employee morale, and I—" He paused, almost as if weighing his words. "I want to be part of that change. I want to help, but there are things you need to understand about me before I can do that."

Emily felt the hairs on the back of her neck stand up. This wasn't just about work anymore. There was something personal in his tone. Something that didn't belong in a boardroom or an HR report.

"Go on," Emily prompted, her voice steady, though her heart was racing.

Julian's eyes briefly flickered with something akin to vulnerability before he quickly masked it with his usual stoic expression. "I can't be part of this company in the way you think I am. I'm not just another employee here, and I never was."

Emily's pulse quickened. There it was again—the cryptic nature, the hints that he was hiding something. But this time, she wasn't going to let him slip away. Not without answers.

"What do you mean?" she asked, leaning forward slightly. She knew she had to tread carefully, but her curiosity had long since overtaken her professional composure.

Julian didn't respond right away. He sat in silence for a moment, staring at the desk in front of him as if gathering his thoughts. Emily could tell he was struggling with something—his past, his identity, his purpose in this world.

"I'm not who you think I am, Ms. Hart," he finally said, his voice quieter now, laced with a hint of regret. "I'm not just some low-level employee trying to make a difference. I've been hiding who I am for a long time, and if you're going to work with me, you need to understand the truth."

Emily's breath caught in her throat. For the first time, she saw the man behind the mask. There was a desperation in his eyes, a quiet plea for understanding. She had no idea what he was about to say, but she knew it would change everything.

Before she could respond, there was a knock at the door. Sarah entered, a clipboard in hand, looking slightly flustered. "Ms. Hart, I'm sorry to interrupt, but there's a problem with the—" She stopped abruptly, noticing Julian sitting there, his gaze fixed on her. "Oh, I didn't realize you were busy…"

Emily glanced at Julian, then back at Sarah. "It's fine, Sarah. Just give me a moment."

Sarah hesitated but nodded and left the room, closing the door behind her.

As the sound of footsteps faded, Emily turned her attention back to Julian. "You were saying?" she prompted, her voice softer now.

He took a deep breath, visibly trying to compose himself. "I'm the owner of this company," he confessed, his words hanging heavily in the air between them. "Julian Sterling... the billionaire. The one everyone knows but no one really sees. I've been hiding under a different name, living in the shadows of my own creation."

Emily's eyes widened, her mind racing to process his words. This man—this elusive figure she had been so intrigued by—was the very one she had been investigating. The owner of Sterling Enterprises, the man whose wealth and status were the subject of so many rumors and speculations. The very man she had unknowingly been working for.

She sat back in her chair, struggling to absorb the magnitude of his revelation. Julian Sterling—the billionaire who had carefully constructed a life of secrecy, a man who hid behind a facade of anonymity. The one person she never expected to meet in her lifetime.

For a long moment, neither of them spoke. The rain outside seemed to intensify, pounding against the windows as if echoing the weight of the conversation that was unfolding. Emily felt as if the ground beneath her was shifting, the world she thought she knew crumbling with every word he spoke.

Finally, she found her voice. "Why?" she whispered. "Why hide?"

Julian's gaze softened, his face weary. "Because, Ms. Hart, the world isn't kind to those like me. I've had enough of being judged for my wealth, for my name. I wanted to be... normal. To live a life where I wasn't always defined by what I own, but by who I am."

And for the first time, Emily saw him—truly saw him—not as the man hiding behind his disguise, but as someone who had been running from his own identity, seeking solace in the shadows.

"I understand," she said quietly, though her mind was spinning. She hadn't expected this truth, hadn't expected to find herself so close to a man who had built a life on secrets.

And just as the silence stretched between them, Emily knew one thing for certain: this was only the beginning.

Three

Behind the Mask

The following days at Sterling Enterprises passed in a blur for Emily. Julian's revelation had left her reeling, her mind unable to fully process the depth of what he had shared. The image of him—cool, distant, a man who had concealed his identity for so long—remained firmly etched in her mind. It wasn't just the shock of discovering that he was the billionaire owner of the company. It was the look in his eyes when he spoke of hiding behind a mask, the raw vulnerability beneath his carefully constructed façade. Something about it stirred something deep within her, making her both sympathetic and intrigued.

She had tried to focus on work, but Julian's confession kept creeping back into her thoughts. What had driven him to live in the shadows? How had he managed to maintain such an elaborate disguise, and for how long? She couldn't help but wonder what lay behind that mask, the part of him that he refused to reveal to anyone.

Every time she passed by his office, she couldn't stop herself from glancing inside, half-expecting to see him there, pretending to be someone else. But Julian was nowhere to be seen. He had stopped attending the usual meetings, and his presence in the office had dwindled. His sudden disappearance only fueled Emily's curiosity. Where was he? What was he hiding? And why was he so determined to keep his real identity buried beneath layers of deception?

It was late one evening when Emily finally found herself at the office after everyone else had gone home. The rain had started to fall again, heavy and unrelenting, casting a grey pallor over the city. She sat at her desk, reviewing reports and trying to catch up on the backlog of work. Her fingers moved mechanically over the keyboard, but her mind was elsewhere, lost in thoughts of Julian and his secrets.

She needed answers. The more she thought about it, the more she felt compelled to uncover the truth. Julian had entrusted her with his secret, and she couldn't just let it go. There was something beneath the surface—something she needed to understand. She couldn't shake the feeling that his past, his life before Sterling Enterprises, was the key to everything.

As if on cue, the door to her office creaked open. Emily looked up, startled, to find Julian standing in the doorway, his figure outlined by the dim light from the hallway. He wasn't wearing the sunglasses this time, and there was no hint of the disguise he had worn the first time they met. He was dressed casually—jeans, a black t-shirt, and a jacket—his usual stoic expression replaced by something more pained.

"Ms. Hart," Julian said quietly, his voice carrying a weight that felt foreign to him. "I need to speak with you."

Emily stood, her heart pounding. She hadn't expected him to show up tonight. The last time they had spoken, he had been distant, unwilling to reveal much about himself. Now, it seemed like he was ready to open up, but something told her that whatever he was about to say would change everything.

"Of course," Emily said, her voice steady but laced with anticipation. She motioned to the chair across from her desk. "Please, have a seat."

Julian walked into the room, his footsteps almost silent against the hardwood floor. He sat down, his posture stiff, his hands folded tightly in his lap as if he were trying to contain some deep turmoil.

"I've been thinking," he began, his voice low and guarded. "About everything I said to you the other day. I wasn't entirely truthful."

Emily's breath hitched, a knot tightening in her stomach. She had known that there was more to the story. There had to be. His confession was just the tip of the iceberg, and now he was admitting that even that wasn't enough.

Behind the Mask

"What do you mean?" she asked, her voice barely above a whisper. She leaned forward slightly, her eyes never leaving his. She had to know what he was hiding.

Julian hesitated, his gaze flickering toward the window before returning to her. "I told you I was hiding behind a mask, but the truth is… it's not just that. It's who I am, what I've done, and the life I've built. It's all a lie."

Emily's heart raced. "A lie?" she echoed, her mind scrambling to keep up with the weight of his words. "What do you mean? What are you hiding, Julian?"

He ran a hand through his hair, his frustration evident as he fought to find the right words. "I've spent years building this company, creating an empire. But it's not the empire I wanted— it's the one I thought I was supposed to have. It's all a mask. A way to hide from my past, from who I really am."

Emily's brow furrowed as she tried to make sense of his cryptic words. "Your past?" she asked. "What past?"

Julian took a deep breath, his eyes closing for a moment as if preparing himself to share something that he had long kept hidden. When he opened them again, they were filled with a sorrow that cut through the hardness of his exterior.

"My real name isn't Julian Sterling," he said quietly. "That's just the persona I created to escape. My real name is Lucas Gray. And I was born into a life that was nothing like this. My family… we weren't wealthy. We didn't have power or influence.

I worked my way up from nothing."

Emily's mind whirled. Lucas Gray. The name felt foreign on his lips, like a ghost that had been buried in the past. "But… why the change? Why the new identity?"

Julian—or rather, Lucas—looked down at his hands, his voice barely above a whisper. "Because I had to. I was running from my past, from my family. They were involved in things… things I didn't want any part of. My father was a criminal, and my mother was… well, she was involved with him. I knew I had to get away, to leave it all behind. I took a new name, a new life, and I built Sterling Enterprises from the ground up."

Emily's breath caught in her throat. She had suspected that there was more to his story, but she hadn't imagined anything like this. Lucas Gray—a man who had risen from the ashes of a broken past, a man who had fought to escape the shadow of his family. And yet, here he was, still haunted by the very thing he had tried to leave behind.

"But why keep it a secret?" Emily asked, her voice trembling slightly. "Why not just tell the truth? You've built an empire. You've made something of yourself."

Lucas's eyes darkened, and there was a bitter laugh in his throat. "Because the truth would destroy everything I've worked for. People don't want to know the real story. They want the polished version, the success story, the one that's easy to accept. If they knew the truth about who I really am… about where I came from… they wouldn't see me the same way. They wouldn't trust me. And worse, they wouldn't believe in Sterling Enterprises anymore."

Emily felt a pang of sympathy for him. She had always admired his drive, his ambition. But now, she saw the cost of that ambition. The weight of a past that would never let him go, no matter how far he ran.

"So you've been hiding behind a mask all this time," Emily said softly, the pieces of the puzzle falling into place. "Living in fear of being discovered. Never allowing anyone to see the real you."

Lucas nodded slowly, his jaw tight. "Exactly. I thought I could outrun it. But the longer I stayed in this disguise, the harder it became to face myself. I've built this company, but I've never truly lived. I've been hiding from my own reflection."

There was a long silence between them, the air thick with unspoken words. Emily could feel the weight of his confession settling into her chest, a sense of understanding washing over her. He wasn't just hiding from the world—he was hiding from himself.

"I understand," she said quietly, her voice calm but filled with emotion. "But you don't have to hide anymore, Lucas. You don't have to keep living behind the mask. You've built something incredible, something people believe in. It's time to let them see the real you."

He looked at her, his eyes searching hers as if trying to gauge her sincerity. For a moment, it felt like everything else faded away—the rain outside, the office, the world. It was just the two of them, standing at the crossroads of truth and deception.

Lucas exhaled slowly, his shoulders sagging with a mixture of relief and exhaustion. "Maybe you're right," he whispered. "Maybe it's time to stop running."

And in that moment, Emily knew that everything was about to change. Behind the mask of Julian Sterling, she had found Lucas Gray. And whatever came next, she knew it would be a journey they would take together.

Four

The Unseen Connection

The office had an eerie quiet that afternoon. The usual sounds of clattering keyboards and hushed conversations had faded into the background, and only the low hum of fluorescent lights filled the space. Emily Hart sat at her desk, her fingers absently tapping the pen against the edge of her notebook. She had tried to focus on her work, but the conversation with Lucas Gray—no longer Julian Sterling—had consumed her thoughts for the better part of the last two days.

It was as if everything she had known about him had been turned upside down. Lucas was not just the billionaire businessman she had imagined, nor was he the man hiding behind a mask to protect his wealth. He was someone far more complex. A man driven by the need to escape his past, to outrun the shadows of his family and their criminal ties. But in his eyes, she had seen something else—a quiet desperation, a longing for freedom, for redemption. And that was something Emily couldn't ignore.

It had been two days since their conversation, and Emily had barely heard from him. After his confession, Lucas had retreated into the shadows once again, as though the weight of his truth had driven him back into the very life he had been trying to escape. The cold, guarded man she had first met—the man who kept his emotions buried—had disappeared, leaving only the fragments of what he had shared with her behind.

Her phone buzzed, breaking her from her thoughts. It was a message from Sarah, her assistant.

"Ms. Hart, Mr. Sterling asked to see you. He wants to meet at the café downstairs in 20 minutes."

Emily's heart skipped a beat. The message was simple, but it held an undercurrent of tension. She hadn't expected to see Lucas today, not after the way they had left things. And yet, the thought of meeting him again sent a rush of anticipation through her. There was unfinished business between them, a connection that neither of them could deny.

She quickly grabbed her jacket and headed out of the office, her mind racing. What could he want to discuss now? Why had he reached out again? Part of her wanted to run away from the situation—she didn't want to get caught up in the complexity of his life, especially after the secrets he had revealed. But another part of her, the part she had tried to suppress, was drawn to him. She couldn't deny the pull. There was something between them, something she couldn't explain. It wasn't just the mystery of his past or the secrets he kept—it was the way he made her feel when he was near. Vulnerable. Alive. As if she was the only person who truly saw him.

The café downstairs was dimly lit, cozy, and smelled of freshly ground coffee and baked goods. The quiet murmur of conversations blended with the soft clink of coffee cups and the occasional whirr of the espresso machine. Emily scanned the room as she entered, her eyes immediately locking onto Lucas, sitting alone at a corner table near the window. He looked out of place there, dressed casually in a dark hoodie and jeans, his hair still slightly tousled as if he hadn't bothered with the meticulous grooming she had come to associate with Julian Sterling.

He didn't notice her approach at first, lost in his thoughts as he stared out the window. Emily hesitated for a moment, her breath catching in her throat. There was something about him now—something raw and exposed. He wasn't the polished businessman she had first met, but a man stripped of his armor, a man trying to reconcile the past with the present. It was a side of him she had never seen, and it made her heart ache.

When she reached his table, he looked up, his expression unreadable. He gave her a small, almost imperceptible nod, motioning for her to sit.

"Thank you for meeting me," he said quietly, his voice carrying a weight she hadn't heard before. There was no trace of the confident, commanding billionaire in his tone—just a man struggling to find his place in a world that had never given him a chance to be himself.

Emily sat down across from him, her heart pounding in her chest. "Of course. What's going on, Lucas? Why did you want to meet?"

Lucas sighed, his fingers curling around the edge of his coffee cup. His eyes flickered with something—something close to regret, but also a deep, lingering sadness. "I've been thinking a lot about what we talked about," he began, his gaze fixed on his hands. "About who I am, who I was, and what I've become. I thought I could leave it all behind, but it's never that simple. The past doesn't just disappear."

Emily leaned forward slightly, her curiosity piqued. "What do you mean? You said you wanted to stop hiding, but it seems like you're still carrying it with you. Whatever it is, it's weighing you down."

He met her gaze then, and for a moment, she saw a flicker of vulnerability in his eyes. It was fleeting, but it was there—just beneath the surface, waiting to break free.

"I thought that by becoming someone else, by building this company, I could erase the past," he said, his voice tight. "But every time I look in the mirror, I see a man who doesn't belong here. A man who can never escape the legacy of his family. And no matter how much I try to hide, it always catches up with me."

The Unseen Connection

Emily's heart ached for him. She had known that there was more to his story, but hearing him speak so openly about his struggles made her realize just how deeply this affected him. This wasn't just about protecting his wealth or reputation—it was about something far more personal. His family, his past, his very identity—everything he had worked for was built on a foundation of lies, and now, it was threatening to crumble.

"Lucas," she said gently, her voice soft but firm, "you don't have to keep carrying that burden alone. You don't have to keep pretending to be someone you're not. I don't know what happened in your past, but I know that you're not the man your family wanted you to be. You've made something of yourself. You've built this empire on your own terms. That matters."

His eyes flickered with something—hope, perhaps, but it was quickly replaced by a shadow of doubt. "But what if it's not enough? What if the past always haunts me, no matter what I do?"

Emily reached across the table, her hand resting gently over his. The contact was electric, and she could feel the tension in his muscles as he stiffened. But she didn't pull away. Instead, she gave his hand a soft, reassuring squeeze. "It's enough," she said, her voice filled with conviction. "You don't need to erase your past, Lucas. You need to confront it. And you don't have to do it alone. I'm here for you."

He stared at her for a long moment, as if trying to understand the sincerity in her words. She saw the struggle in his eyes, the battle between the man he had been forced to become and the man he wanted to be. But something in his gaze softened, and for the first time, he allowed himself to believe that maybe, just maybe, he wasn't beyond saving.

"I don't know what I've done to deserve your support," he murmured, his voice barely above a whisper. "But I'm grateful for it."

Emily smiled softly, her heart swelling with a warmth she hadn't expected. "You don't need to earn it, Lucas. You just need to be yourself."

For the first time in a long while, Lucas Gray—the man who had spent years hiding behind a mask—looked at her with something akin to hope. There was still much to be done, still many demons to face, but for the first time, it felt like the weight on his shoulders had lightened, if only for a moment.

As they sat there in the dimly lit café, the rain continuing to pour outside, Emily realized that something had shifted between them. It wasn't just about the mystery of his past or the secrets he kept—it was about the connection that had formed between them, the bond that had been forged through honesty and vulnerability. They were no longer just two people trapped in their own lives—they were two souls, drawn together by their shared pain and the desire to find a way forward.

The path ahead was uncertain, but Emily knew one thing for sure: she wasn't going to let Lucas walk it alone. And as their hands remained entwined on the table, she could feel the weight of that unspoken promise settling between them—a promise to face whatever came next, together.

Five

Connection

The days that followed the meeting at the café felt different—darker, charged with an energy Emily hadn't been prepared for. She had stepped into this relationship with a sense of professionalism, a curiosity about the man behind the mask. What started as a simple professional connection had evolved into something far deeper, something far more complicated. She couldn't stop thinking about Lucas. About what he had shared, the vulnerability that had taken over him that night. His past had begun to pull at her like an unrelenting current, drawing her deeper into the mystery of the man who could never seem to let go.

Emily wasn't naïve. She knew the world was never kind to those who sought to outrun their pasts, who lived with constant fear of discovery. But Lucas was different from everyone she had known. His need to hide was palpable, a shadow that loomed over everything he did. She couldn't help but wonder what would happen when the inevitable came—when someone discovered the truth he so desperately wanted to bury.

She spent her days in the office, her thoughts often drifting to Lucas. He had started showing up again, but it wasn't the same. He was more withdrawn, colder in his interactions, and the mask he had so carefully crafted seemed to have become even thicker. It was almost as if the weight of their last conversation had driven him further into himself, locking away the parts of him she had started to see—the parts that were real.

It was one late evening, the kind where the world outside was shrouded in the dark blue of night, when Emily got a call from an unknown number. She hesitated before answering, unsure whether it was business or something else, but something told her this was important. Something told her it was about Lucas.

"Hello?"

"Emily," his voice came through, strained, almost like a whisper carried through the phone. "I need to see you. Now."

Her heart rate spiked. The urgency in his tone sent a chill down her spine. This wasn't just a casual request. This was different. "Lucas?" she asked, trying to steady her voice. "What's going on? What's happened?"

There was a long pause, filled only by the faint sound of his breathing, a rhythmic sound that almost made her think he was holding his breath. When he spoke again, it was softer, almost as though he was afraid of being overheard. "I... I think it's time. I can't keep hiding anymore. There's something you need to know."

The words hung in the air, unspoken and heavy. Emily felt a wave of panic roll through her. What was he talking about? What was so important that he felt the need to reach out now, after all this time?

"Where are you?" she asked quickly, her voice sharp with concern.

"I'll text you the address," he replied, and before she could respond, the line went dead.

Emily stared at her phone for a moment, her heart thudding loudly in her chest. Her mind raced, the unanswered questions multiplying like wildfire. She quickly checked her messages, and sure enough, there was a text from him with an address, followed by a short message: Please, just trust me.

Without thinking, Emily grabbed her coat and rushed out the door. The office had emptied long ago, and the streets were quiet, save for the occasional car passing by. The rain had started again, drizzling lightly against her face, as if the world outside was trying to mirror her unease. She didn't know what to expect, didn't know what Lucas was about to reveal. But something in her gut told her that whatever it was, it was big. Bigger than anything she had ever imagined.

The address Lucas had sent her led her to a quiet part of the city, an area that seemed far removed from the bustling life of the corporate world she knew so well. She pulled up to a small building, a nondescript apartment complex that seemed ordinary enough at first glance, but there was something off about it—something that made her feel like she was walking into a different world altogether.

When she rang the buzzer, the door clicked open almost immediately. It was as though someone had been waiting for her. She stepped inside, and the hallway felt unusually silent. The faint smell of old wood and dust hung in the air, the dim lights flickering overhead. It wasn't a place you would expect to find someone like Lucas. It wasn't a place where someone as powerful as the billionaire owner of Sterling Enterprises would ever choose to be.

She walked up the narrow stairs, each step echoing in the silence. At the top, she found the door he had described, its number barely visible in the dim light. She knocked softly, unsure what to expect. But when the door opened, Lucas stood there, his eyes dark with something she couldn't quite place. There was a tension in the air, something heavy that seemed to cling to him like a second skin.

"Come in," he said, his voice low, almost strained.

She stepped inside, and the first thing she noticed was the state of the apartment. It was sparsely furnished—just a few chairs, a small table, and the faint scent of stale cigarettes. But it was the photographs on the wall that caught her attention. They were old, black-and-white photos, faded with age. In each of them, Lucas was a boy, a teenager, standing next to people who looked far too familiar.

Her breath caught in her throat.

They were photographs of him with people she had seen before—his family, no doubt. But these weren't just any family portraits. They were images of power—images of a world she had only heard whispers about. The kind of world that existed in the shadows, hidden from public view.

Lucas saw her staring at the photos and sighed heavily. "I didn't want you to see this, but I don't have a choice anymore."

He walked over to a cabinet and retrieved a small box from the shelf. It was made of wood, old and weathered, and when he opened it, Emily saw what lay inside: a collection of documents. Legal papers, financial records, and newspaper clippings—all of them connected to a name that sent a chill down her spine.

The Gray family.

"I've been running from this," Lucas said quietly, his eyes filled with a mix of regret and resolve. "I told you I left my past behind, but the truth is, I never could. I've spent my entire life pretending to be someone I'm not—hiding behind Julian Sterling, hiding behind a company I built with the hopes of escaping this. But this—" He gestured toward the box, "—this is who I really am. This is the legacy I'm trying to outrun."

Emily's pulse quickened as she scanned the documents. She

could feel the weight of them—the weight of everything Lucas had tried to escape. But what was worse was the realization that whatever this legacy was, it was something far more dangerous than just family secrets.

"What happened, Lucas?" she asked, her voice barely above a whisper. "What is this? What does all of this mean?"

He turned to her, his expression hardening as though the very mention of his past brought pain too deep to share. "My father wasn't just a businessman, Emily. He was a criminal—an infamous one. He built his empire on illegal activities, on extortion, manipulation, and violence. I tried to escape it. I thought that if I left everything behind, I could start fresh. But the truth is, it never leaves you. It follows you. It destroys everything you try to build."

Emily took a step forward, her heart pounding in her chest. "So, what does this mean for you? For Sterling Enterprises?"

Lucas's eyes were dark with emotion, the weight of his confession bearing down on him. "I'm being watched. People know who I really am. They know my past, and they won't let me forget it. My father's enemies, his associates—they've been waiting for me to slip up, to make a mistake. They know I'm vulnerable, and now they're coming for me. They want what's mine. They want everything I've built."

The gravity of his words settled in her chest like a stone. She hadn't realized just how deep his connection to the past went, how dangerous it truly was. And now, it wasn't just Lucas who was at risk—it was the entire company, everything he had worked for, and everyone who had ever placed their trust in him.

"You're not alone in this," Emily said, her voice strong, even though her mind was reeling. "We'll figure this out. We'll get through it together."

Lucas's gaze softened, the weight of his years of hiding finally starting to lift. For the first time, Emily saw the true depth of his vulnerability—his fear not just for himself, but for the people he cared about.

"I don't know how much longer I can keep running, Emily," he whispered. "But I'll fight. I'll fight for the life I've built. And for you."

In that moment, the connection between them—real and raw—solidified. She wasn't just standing with him in his fight; she was with him, fully and completely, ready to face whatever darkness his past might bring. Together, they would confront the demons that had haunted him for so long. Together, they would fight to keep the world they had built from crumbling around them.

Six

Love

The following morning, the office was filled with the usual energy—a dull hum of phones ringing, people moving between departments, the occasional bursts of laughter echoing in the hallways. But Emily couldn't shake the heaviness that clung to her from the night before. The conversation with Lucas had left an indelible mark on her, one she couldn't escape. The revelations he had shared, the glimpse into his fractured past, still swirled in her mind like a storm she couldn't quiet. He had asked her for help, for her trust, and now everything she thought she knew about her life—about herself—was being torn apart.

It was one thing to sympathize with someone's pain, to listen to their story. But it was entirely different to become entwined in that story, to step into the unknown with someone who had so much to lose. She had already seen the way his past had shaped him, the way it had twisted his view of the world and how he saw himself. And yet, there was a part of her that couldn't let go, couldn't walk away. Because behind that mask of a man so desperate to outrun his legacy, she had seen the real Lucas. And for better or worse, she was already too deep to turn back now.

Her phone buzzed on her desk, cutting through the tension that had settled in her chest. The message was from Lucas.

"We need to meet again. Tonight. Same place. I have something important to tell you."

Her fingers hovered over the screen, uncertainty washing over her. What could he possibly have to say now? What more was there to reveal? She didn't know if she was ready for whatever came next, but she couldn't deny that she was drawn to him. Whatever the consequences were, she was in it now—whether she liked it or not.

Emily had learned long ago that curiosity wasn't always a gift. It could be a curse, too. And now, as she stood up to leave her office, preparing to meet him again, she could feel the weight of the unknown pressing down on her.

The café from the night before was quieter now, as the evening settled over the city. The usual clinking of cups and quiet chatter had been replaced by a solemn hush. As she entered, she saw Lucas seated at the same corner table, his back to the window, but his eyes were locked on the door as if he had been waiting for her all along. She could see the strain in his posture, the tightness in his jaw, but there was something else too—something darker. It was a look she had seen before, but never on him. The look of a man who had come to terms with something he couldn't undo.

"Lucas," Emily said softly, walking over to his table. "What's going on?"

He didn't immediately respond. Instead, he motioned for her to sit, his eyes still fixed on something far away. The air between them felt thick, heavier than the last time. There was no warmth in his smile, no assurance that everything would be okay. There was only a quiet, almost suffocating tension that pressed down on them both.

"I've been thinking," he started, his voice low, each word like it was weighing him down. "About everything. About us. About how deep this has gone. And I need you to understand something, Emily—something I should've told you a long time ago."

His eyes met hers then, the rawness in them making her stomach flip. It was a look that told her this wasn't going to be a simple conversation. This wasn't going to be a resolution. Whatever he had to say would change everything.

"Go on," she said, trying to steady her breath, but the growing dread in her chest made it difficult.

"The truth is, I've always known that getting involved with someone like you... someone who doesn't know the whole story, who doesn't understand the dangers that come with being connected to me, was a mistake." His voice cracked slightly, and for the first time, Emily saw the cracks in his armor. "But I couldn't help myself. I couldn't walk away. And now... now I'm dragging you into it too."

Emily shook her head, not understanding. "What are you talking about? Lucas, this is not your fault. You didn't ask for this. I—"

"No." His interruption was sharp, cutting through her words. "I did. I asked for this. And it's going to cost you. It's going to cost both of us. Because the moment I let you in, the moment I let anyone close, I've made us both targets. And I don't think you understand just how dangerous that is."

The words hung in the air, making her throat tighten. A target. Her mind raced, but she couldn't find the thread of logic to hold onto. She had thought he had confessed everything. She had thought she understood the weight of his past, the darkness that followed him, but now, it seemed like there was more. There was always more.

"What do you mean by that?" Emily asked, her voice barely a whisper. The unease she had been trying to suppress now bubbled to the surface, threatening to drown her. "What's really going on, Lucas?"

He met her gaze, and she could see the fear in his eyes now—the same fear she had felt when he told her about his family, about the legacy he was trying to escape. But now, it was different. There was a heaviness in the air, something more tangible than before, something that felt... final.

"I've been involved in things I shouldn't have," he began, his voice shaky now. "My father's enemies... they never left. They've been waiting for me to make a mistake, to show a weakness, and now they're circling. They know about you, Emily. They know about us. They've been watching me for weeks. And now... they're coming for you."

Her heart skipped a beat. The world seemed to tilt on its axis as the weight of his words sank in. They were being watched? All this time, he had been hiding his identity, running from a past he could never escape—and now, that past had found them.

"Lucas, I—I don't understand," Emily stammered, her mind struggling to catch up. "What does this mean for us? For me?"

"It means they won't stop," he said, his voice steady but filled with an intensity that sent chills down her spine. "They'll do whatever it takes to get to me, to destroy everything I've built. And if you're connected to me, they'll use you as leverage. They'll hurt you, Emily. And I won't let that happen."

For the first time, Emily felt the full weight of what she was involved in. This wasn't just about love or the allure of a man who had a troubled past—it was about survival. She had known it in her gut, had felt the undercurrent of danger since the moment Lucas had opened up to her. But now, it was real. They were being hunted, both of them, and she didn't know what to do, how to make it stop.

"But I don't want to walk away," Emily said, her voice trembling but resolute. "I'm not afraid of you, Lucas. I'm not afraid of us."

He reached out then, his hand covering hers, his touch desperate, pleading. "Emily, you don't know what they're capable of. I've tried to protect you from this, but it's too late. There's nothing I can do to keep you safe anymore. And if you stay—if you stay with me, you're going to pay the price."

The air between them thickened as the full weight of his words settled over her. This wasn't just about love anymore. It was about survival. And as she looked into his eyes, she knew that the life they could have had—the life they dreamed of, together— was slipping through their fingers like sand. They had been naive to think they could escape this. That they could outrun the darkness.

"Is there a way out?" Emily asked, her voice barely above a whisper. "Can we fight back? Can we end this before it gets worse?"

Lucas's eyes clouded with regret. "I wish I could tell you there's an easy way out. But the truth is, there's no escape. Not for me, not for you."

And in that moment, Emily understood. The price of loving Lucas Gray was higher than she could have ever imagined. It wasn't just her heart on the line. It was her life.

And as the shadows of their past closed in around them, she realized that the love she had found—so unexpected, so raw—

Love

had come at a cost that neither of them were ready to pay.

Seven

Another Life

The night was heavy, thick with rain that clung to the pavement like the weight of a thousand secrets. Emily's car cut through the slick streets, headlights slicing through the darkness. Her mind buzzed, a whirlwind of confusion and fear. She had left Lucas's apartment an hour ago, her heart pounding in her chest, her thoughts spinning faster than she could process.

The words he had spoken to her—the words about the people who were now watching them, the ones who had tracked them down, who had known about them before they even realized it—echoed in her mind. They weren't just running from his past anymore. They were running from something that could destroy them both.

Her grip tightened on the steering wheel as she tried to focus, but the city around her felt unreal, like it was fading away, the very ground beneath her feet starting to feel unsteady. She had heard of men like Lucas before—the ones who got too deep, who made too many enemies, and who paid the price for it in ways that no one could ever expect. But Lucas wasn't just anyone. He wasn't just a businessman, a man with power and influence. He was a man with a dangerous past, one that had the potential to ruin everything he had built.

And now, it was threatening to ruin her, too.

She pulled up to her apartment building, the familiar structure looming ahead, a sanctuary that now felt like a prison. She had tried to push everything that had happened out of her mind, but the weight of Lucas's confession had anchored itself deep inside her. He had told her that there was no way out, that there was nothing they could do to stop the inevitable. But Emily wasn't ready to accept that. She couldn't just walk away from him, from them. The connection between them was too strong, too real. She couldn't let go—not yet.

She parked her car and sat for a moment, staring at the building in front of her, the distant sound of thunder rumbling in the distance. The rain pelted against the windows as if the world was trying to wash away the past, to cleanse everything that had led them to this point.

The phone in her hand buzzed, jolting her from her thoughts. It was a message from Lucas.

"Stay inside. Don't go anywhere. I'll explain everything soon.

Trust me."

Her thumb hovered over the screen, but she didn't know how to respond. She didn't know what to say. She wasn't sure who she could trust anymore. The man she had known—the one she had fallen for—was disappearing before her eyes. And in his place was someone she didn't recognize. Someone broken, desperate, and ready to sacrifice everything to keep her safe.

She opened the door and stepped out into the rain, the cold droplets seeping through her clothes. As she reached the building's entrance, she noticed a figure standing in the shadows just beyond the streetlamp's glow. For a moment, she froze, her heart skipping a beat.

But then she recognized him.

It was Lucas.

Her breath caught in her throat, and she rushed forward, but as she drew closer, she saw the tension in his posture. His shoulders were rigid, his hands clenched at his sides. His eyes, usually so guarded, were wide and panicked, like a man on the edge of something he couldn't control.

"Lucas," she whispered, her voice shaky, filled with worry. "What's happening?"

He didn't answer at first. Instead, he pulled her toward the door, urging her inside, away from the rain. Once they were in the lobby, he glanced over his shoulder, as if expecting someone to be following them.

"Listen to me, Emily," he said, his voice low and urgent. "You need to stay calm, and you need to listen carefully. There are people after me—after us. They know we've been in contact, and they won't stop until they have what they want. I've already put you in danger by letting you get this close. I thought I could protect you, but I was wrong."

Emily's mind raced. She had known something like this was coming, but hearing the words from his lips was different. It made it real, it made it undeniable. She had been right to feel the weight of it all. But she wasn't about to back down now—not when she knew how deep this ran.

"Who are they, Lucas?" she asked, her voice steady despite the fear that threatened to overwhelm her. "What do they want?"

Lucas didn't answer immediately. Instead, he ran a hand through his wet hair, frustration and helplessness evident on his face. "They want control. My father's old associates—they've been waiting for the moment when I would slip up. They want what's mine. They'll stop at nothing to get it. And now they want you, too."

Emily swallowed hard. This was worse than she had imagined. It wasn't just a family vendetta; this was something much bigger, something that could cost them both their lives.

"Why didn't you tell me sooner?" she asked, the words escaping her before she could stop them. "Why didn't you trust me?"

Lucas closed his eyes, his jaw tightening. "I didn't want you to get involved. I thought I could protect you from it—keep you safe. But now, I see I was fooling myself. You're already in this, whether I want you to be or not. And there's nothing I can do to fix it."

A chill ran down Emily's spine. She had felt like she was walking a fine line for days now, but this—this was the moment when everything shifted. When there was no turning back. She was already too deep, and the consequences of that were becoming clearer by the second.

"Lucas, we can't just sit here and wait for them to come for us," Emily said, her voice shaking with urgency. "We have to do something. We can't just let them win."

He turned to face her then, his expression hard, his eyes filled with something she couldn't quite read. "What do you suggest we do? Fight them? Do you think we can win this battle? Do you think you can just walk away from all of this, from everything that's been set in motion?" He took a step closer, his voice lowering to a dangerous whisper. "They'll come for you. They'll come for everything you love, and they won't stop until they've destroyed it all. This is bigger than you, bigger than me."

She felt a surge of anger, of frustration. He was trying to protect her, but it wasn't his choice to make. She wasn't some delicate flower to be shielded from the world—she was a part of this, whether he liked it or not. And she wasn't going to let him shut her out now, not when the stakes had never been higher.

"No," she said, her voice firm, her eyes locking with his. "I won't let you do this alone. You're not the only one who's in danger here. If they want to take everything from us, then we're going to fight back. Together."

Lucas studied her for a moment, and for the first time since this whole nightmare began, something like hope flickered in his eyes. It was fleeting, but it was there—just enough to remind her that he was still the man she had fallen for, the man who hadn't given up on her, on them.

"You really mean that?" he asked quietly, his voice almost a whisper.

Emily nodded, her heart pounding in her chest. "I do."

For a long moment, they stood there, locked in a silent understanding. They both knew that what they were about to face would change everything, that the road ahead would be filled with dangers they couldn't anticipate. But at that moment, with the rain still beating down outside and the weight of the world pressing in around them, Emily knew one thing for certain: she wasn't going to let fear control her. She wasn't going to let it tear them apart.

"Then let's do it," Lucas said, his voice steady now, determination flooding his words. "Let's take the fight to them."

And as they turned to face the storm ahead, Emily knew that nothing would ever be the same again. The shadows of another life were closing in, but together, they would face them head-on, no matter the cost.

Eight

Watchers

The night felt endless, a void that seemed to stretch far beyond the limits of time. Emily stood by the window of her apartment, the cool breeze drifting in from the cracked glass, as she stared out at the city lights below. They shimmered in the distance like fractured stars, beautiful but unreachable. She had always found solace in the view—the hum of the city, the soft murmur of life beneath her feet. But tonight, it felt suffocating, as though the very air around her was closing in.

Beside her, Lucas paced restlessly, his movements sharp, deliberate. Every now and then, he would pause and glance at the door as if expecting it to open, as if someone might be standing there, watching. But no one was. Not yet.

The unease had settled deep inside her, gnawing at her every thought. What was it about his past, about the people who hunted him, that made them so relentless? And why had they decided now, after all this time, that it was finally time to strike?

She could feel the heaviness of his gaze on her, even without looking. He was worried, desperate to protect her, and it made her wonder what he had done—what lengths he had gone to in order to shield her from the inevitable. But as much as she wanted to comfort him, to tell him everything would be alright, she knew the truth. They were past the point of safety. There was no easy way out, no hidden doors that would lead them into the light.

It was only a matter of time before the storm broke.

"Emily," Lucas's voice cut through the silence, pulling her back to the present. She turned to face him, her heart heavy in her chest. "I need to tell you something else. Something you have to understand before it's too late."

She held his gaze, her breath caught in her throat. Every instinct told her to back away, to demand he explain what he meant, but she couldn't. She had already stepped too far into this world, and there was no turning back.

"What is it?" she asked softly, though her voice betrayed the tension that twisted inside her.

His eyes darkened, and for a moment, he seemed like a different man—someone who had carried the weight of too many secrets for too long. "There's more to this than just my family," he said, his voice tight with urgency. "These people, the ones who've been hunting me—they're not just criminals. They're part of something much bigger. A network, a system, that goes deeper than I ever realized."

Emily's brow furrowed, her mind racing. She stepped closer to him, trying to piece together the fragments of information he had already shared with her. "A network? What do you mean?"

"They're connected to global operations, to organized crime syndicates that span continents," Lucas continued, his words tumbling out with a mix of frustration and fear. "My father wasn't just a kingpin in one city or one country. He was a part of something international. And when I ran, when I built this life, I thought I could escape it all. But I was wrong. These people—they've been watching me for years. They've been waiting for me to make a mistake."

Emily felt a chill run down her spine. The implications of what Lucas was saying were terrifying. "But why now? Why are they coming for us now?"

Lucas ran a hand through his hair, his eyes haunted. "Because I've crossed a line. I've started making moves, cutting off connections, going after people who are too deeply entrenched. They've seen me as a threat for a while now, and now they know I'm vulnerable. That's why they've targeted you, Emily. They know that if they hurt you, if they break you, they'll break me."

The weight of his words sank in like lead in her chest. It wasn't just the danger they faced. It wasn't just his past that had come back to haunt them. It was the fact that they were both standing at the center of a storm they couldn't outrun, a storm that had been brewing for years.

"I don't care about what they want from me, Lucas," Emily said, her voice firm despite the fear gnawing at her. "I'm not going to let them control me, control us. We can fight back. We have to."

He looked at her, his expression softening for the briefest of moments. But then his gaze darkened again, and she saw the conflict in his eyes. "It's not that simple. You don't understand what they're capable of. These people—they're not just dangerous. They're everywhere. They have eyes and ears in places we can't even imagine."

Suddenly, the doorbell rang.

Both of them froze.

The sound echoed through the apartment, jarring in its finality. For a moment, neither of them moved. The world seemed to hold its breath. Then, without a word, Lucas went to the door, his footsteps quiet but urgent. Emily's heart thudded in her chest, her pulse racing. Every instinct told her to run, to hide. But there was nowhere to go. They were trapped in the middle of a game they didn't fully understand, and no matter how much they fought, no matter how much they tried to outsmart the people chasing them, it would never be enough.

Lucas hesitated at the door, his hand hovering over the knob.

He looked back at Emily, his face pale, his jaw clenched. There was no time to prepare. No time to hide.

"I need you to stay back," he said quietly, his voice tense. "Do not open the door. Do not make a sound."

Emily nodded, her heart in her throat. She backed away, stepping into the shadows, her mind racing as she tried to prepare herself for whatever was about to happen.

Lucas opened the door slowly, just a crack, peering through the narrow gap. His face remained expressionless, but his eyes narrowed as he spoke.

"Can I help you?" he asked, his voice calm, but there was a cold edge to it, one that made Emily's blood run cold.

There was a pause on the other side of the door, then a voice—a low, gravelly voice—spoke.

"We've been watching you, Mr. Gray," it said, and Emily's stomach dropped. "It's time to end this charade."

Before Lucas could react, the door burst open with a force that sent him stumbling back. Two figures rushed into the room—men in dark suits, their movements fast and practiced. They were like shadows, quick and silent, and their presence filled the room with an almost tangible sense of threat.

"Emily," one of them said, his voice low and cold, his eyes locking onto hers with a predatory gaze. "You've been a thorn in our side for too long."

Lucas moved quickly, placing himself between Emily and the men, his body tense, his fists clenched. "Stay back," he warned, his voice deadly calm.

The men laughed, a hollow, mocking sound. "You think you can stop us?" the other man sneered. "You're nothing but a runaway, Lucas. A ghost. And this is where you disappear."

Emily's pulse raced. Her mind scrambled for a plan, for an escape, for something—anything—that would give them a chance. But she couldn't think. The fear was too overwhelming.

But then Lucas spoke, his voice steady, his words full of something Emily hadn't heard from him before—defiance.

"You've underestimated me," he said coldly, stepping forward. "You've underestimated both of us."

Before the men could react, Lucas lunged, knocking one of them off balance. The other man reached for something in his jacket, but Lucas was faster. The room erupted into chaos—shouts, the sound of furniture crashing to the floor, the loud thud of fists meeting flesh.

Emily scrambled back, her heart pounding in her chest, as she watched the scene unfold. She didn't know what to do, how to help. She was caught between fear and the desire to fight for Lucas, to protect him. But in that moment, she realized that the fight was bigger than either of them. They weren't just up against men in suits—they were up against a network, a machine, one that wouldn't stop until they were both gone.

As the struggle continued, the men grew more desperate. One of them managed to get the upper hand, throwing Lucas against the wall with brutal force. Emily gasped, rushing to his side, but the man's cold, calculating eyes turned toward her.

"It's over," he said, his voice low and final. "You've made a mistake by getting involved with him. Now, you'll pay the price."

As the darkness closed in, Emily knew one thing for certain—there was no turning back. The world they had built together had already crumbled, and now, the real battle was just beginning. The watchers of the rift had made their move. And neither she nor Lucas had any idea what would happen next.

Nine

Reality

The world felt like it was spinning, a blur of motion and sound that pushed against her senses, a pulse of chaos she couldn't control. The sharp scent of sweat and blood filled the air as Emily knelt beside Lucas, her hands trembling as she tried to keep the pressure on the cut above his eyebrow. The blood had stopped flowing, but the memory of what had happened lingered like a nightmare she couldn't wake from.

The men in the suits had been swift, merciless. She had watched in horror as Lucas fought back, his body moving like a machine, precise, calculating. But even he had limits. And when one of the men had grabbed a gun from his jacket, it all had spiraled out of control. The fact that Lucas had been fast enough to disarm him before anyone was seriously hurt didn't ease the weight of the terror that had gripped Emily's heart. She wasn't

Reality

sure if she was more afraid for Lucas or herself, but as she held his head in her lap, a quiet understanding settled deep within her. This was real now.

She wasn't just a bystander. This wasn't some distant story of a man and his demons. This was her life now—her life with Lucas, and the price they were both paying for it.

"Lucas..." Her voice cracked, the fear laced in her words. "Please. Stay with me."

His eyes fluttered, the blood loss making him weak, but his voice was a whisper, hoarse and strained. "I'm... I'm not going anywhere," he said, his hand weakly gripping hers. "They won't... win."

Emily swallowed hard, her heart hammering in her chest as she tried to steady herself. This wasn't the time for fear. Not now. But all she could think of was how far they had fallen, how deep into this nightmare they had sunk. They had no more time for games. The forces that were after them were too powerful, too pervasive. The entire world was against them now, and the only thing that could save them was finding a way out, fast.

Her mind raced as she heard the faint sound of sirens in the distance. The battle had been loud, messy. She knew it wouldn't be long before the authorities showed up, and with them, more problems. More people who wouldn't care about the reasons behind the violence, only that the bloodshed was there, undeniable and loud. They would come for Lucas, and they would stop at nothing to take him down.

"No, no, no," Emily muttered under her breath, her hands shaking as she tried to help him to his feet. She couldn't lose him. Not now. Not after everything they'd gone through. "We have to go. We can't stay here."

Lucas groaned, his body barely able to hold itself upright as she supported him. His movements were slow, deliberate, but there was an intensity in his eyes that hadn't been there before. The fire that had been buried beneath his surface was now burning bright, more furious than ever.

"We'll leave the city," Lucas said, his voice faint but filled with determination. "There's an old safe house, out on the outskirts. I can't stay here. Not anymore."

Emily didn't argue. She nodded, her mind working at lightning speed, calculating their next steps. But they couldn't just leave, not without more than a few scraps of supplies. She needed to make sure they were prepared, that they had everything they needed to disappear for good. Her pulse quickened as she glanced around the apartment, her eyes landing on the half-packed duffel bag by the door. There was no time to second-guess. No time for mistakes.

"Okay," she said, her voice firm, though her stomach twisted with anxiety. "We'll go. But we have to hurry."

Lucas nodded, slowly getting to his feet with her help. Every step seemed to cost him, his face pale, his breath shallow. He was struggling, but Emily refused to let him collapse. Not now. Not when they had so little time.

Reality

She glanced at the door, feeling the weight of every second pressing against them. If they didn't leave now, it would be too late. The world was closing in. The walls of their existence were tightening, forcing them into a corner from which there was no escape.

With a final look around the apartment, Emily grabbed the bag, slinging it over her shoulder. She grabbed her phone, eyes scanning the screen quickly. No missed calls. No messages. But that didn't mean anything. They were being watched—tracked—and every minute they wasted meant another chance for someone to catch up with them.

"You ready?" she asked, her voice tight.

Lucas's eyes met hers, and for a split second, Emily saw something there—something deep in the shadows of his gaze. It wasn't just fear. It was acceptance. He had come to terms with what they were facing, and now, he was ready.

"I'm ready," he said, his voice steady.

Together, they stepped toward the door, and Emily's heart skipped a beat when she heard the sound of a car pulling up outside. They weren't alone anymore.

"They've found us," Lucas whispered, his eyes narrowing, but there was no panic in his voice. Only resolve.

Emily's pulse spiked as she stepped back, reaching for the gun Lucas had kept hidden in his coat pocket. He had been ready for this, prepared for every eventuality. But now, it was real. She could feel the cold metal of the weapon in her hand, its weight unfamiliar, yet somehow comforting. She wasn't used to this world, to the violence and danger, but she wasn't going to let Lucas fall. Not again.

She raised her finger to her lips, signaling for him to stay silent. He nodded, understanding the urgency in her movement. He could barely stand, let alone fight, but Emily knew he was still dangerous. Still capable. They both were.

The door was still open, the shadows from outside creeping into the room. The sirens were louder now, almost deafening as they screeched closer, and Emily could hear footsteps approaching the building, their owners moving swiftly, purposefully. There was no time to waste. No time to think.

"Get down," Lucas muttered, pushing Emily to the floor. He collapsed beside her, his hand reaching for the gun in her hand.

"I can't let you do this alone," she said through gritted teeth, her voice barely above a whisper.

But Lucas shook his head, his breath ragged. "You have to, Emily. I've already dragged you into this. But you can't fight this battle. Not like I can."

Her eyes flashed with frustration, but she didn't argue. Not now. Not when their lives were hanging in the balance. She could feel it. The walls were closing in, and there was no escape. No way out. Not unless they acted fast.

Reality

The door was getting closer. The men outside were almost at the threshold. Emily's heart raced as she clutched the gun tighter, steeling herself for what was about to come. They wouldn't stop. They wouldn't let them go. And she had no idea if they were strong enough to survive this.

The first man entered the apartment, his silhouette cutting through the dim light of the hallway. Emily barely had time to react before Lucas shot forward, moving faster than she had ever seen him before, despite the blood loss. With a swift, practiced motion, he fired once, the sound echoing through the apartment like a thunderclap. The man crumpled to the floor, but the other men were close behind. Emily's heart raced. She couldn't let up. Not for a second.

She raised the gun, pulling the trigger, and the room seemed to explode in a haze of chaos. The men weren't prepared for her—none of them were—and that gave her the upper hand, for now. But the question still lingered, hanging in the air like smoke.

How much longer could they keep running?

The world outside was changing. The life they had known, the life Emily had wanted, was slipping through her fingers, like sand that refused to stay in one place. She wasn't just fighting to stay alive. She was fighting for something bigger—fighting for the chance to live, to breathe, to love.

But in this world, love came at a price. And that price was more than either of them had ever imagined.

The men outside had been silenced, but Emily knew—she knew—that they wouldn't stop coming. The storm was only beginning. And as Lucas steadied himself beside her, his eyes wild with urgency, Emily realized one thing: there was no way out. There was no turning back. And they were falling through reality, together, with nothing but each other to hold on to.

Ten

The Cost

⚜

The city was a ghost town at this hour. Once teeming with life, the streets now lay silent under the weight of the rain that had continued its relentless assault since the night before. The soft hiss of tyres against wet pavement was the only sound that accompanied them as Lucas and Emily sped through the dark streets, their car's headlights cutting through the mist like twin blades. The world outside was a blur of lights and shadows, everything moving too fast, too close, as if the city itself was pressing in on them.

Emily's breath was shallow as she sat in the passenger seat, her hands clutching the seatbelt as if it were the only thing holding her to reality. Her mind had yet to catch up to the events that had unfolded in the last few hours, and every passing moment felt like a fragmented memory, too sharp to be ignored but too hazy to fully comprehend.

The adrenaline still coursed through her veins, her heart pounding in time with the rhythm of the engine. Lucas, ever the stoic figure beside her, was driving with a precision she had come to expect of him, but the tension in his jaw, the subtle tremor in his hands as they gripped the steering wheel, told her that he, too, was struggling to keep control.

They had left the apartment in a hurry, with little more than the clothes on their backs and a hastily packed bag containing only the essentials. The safe house Lucas had mentioned, the one he had hidden away in the outskirts of the city, was their only hope now. It was the one place where they could regroup, where they could breathe, but even as they sped away from the chaos, Emily couldn't shake the feeling that it wasn't enough.

They weren't safe yet. Not by a long shot.

"Are you sure you're okay?" Lucas's voice broke the silence, quiet but insistent, and Emily turned to look at him. His eyes were fixed on the road ahead, but there was something in the way he spoke that made her feel like he was asking more than just about her physical well-being.

"I'm fine," she replied, her voice steadier than she felt. "Just... just trying to process everything."

The words sounded hollow, even to her own ears. How could she process it? How could she make sense of a world that had shattered into so many jagged pieces? They had almost died tonight. She had almost lost him.

The Cost

Lucas's hand briefly brushed against hers, a fleeting contact that sent a shiver through her. His fingers were warm, but they trembled slightly as if the same storm that raged outside was caught somewhere deep inside him as well. He didn't speak again, but Emily didn't need him to. The silence between them was filled with the weight of unspoken understanding.

They had made it this far, but neither of them had any illusions about how much further they could go.

Emily's phone buzzed in her pocket, the sound sharp and invasive in the quiet of the car. She fumbled for it, her heart racing as she pulled it out and unlocked the screen. The message was from Sarah, her assistant.

"They know. They've found the apartment. They'll be here soon. Get to the safe house. Don't trust anyone. Be careful."

The words hit her like a punch to the gut. They hadn't even reached the safe house yet, and already the walls were closing in. The people who were after Lucas—after them—weren't just dangerous. They were thorough. They had eyes everywhere. There was nowhere to hide. No place that would be truly safe.

"Lucas," she said, her voice breaking through the tension in the car. "They know. They found the apartment. We're not safe yet."

His jaw tightened at the news, but he didn't flinch, didn't even take his eyes off the road. "I know," he said flatly. "They're always one step ahead. We can't outrun them forever."

The words stung. They were trapped. They could run, hide, fight back—but it would never be enough. As long as they were in this game, there would always be someone watching, someone hunting them. And at the heart of it all, the cost of this life was too high to ignore. They were running not just from his past, but from their future.

The safe house loomed ahead, a dilapidated building on the outskirts of the city. It wasn't much—a two-story structure hidden behind a tangle of overgrown ivy and shadowed trees. The windows were dark, and the front door was locked, but it was a place no one had known about for years. It was as close to sanctuary as they could get.

Lucas pulled up to the house, parking the car a few yards away. He cut the engine, and the silence between them settled in like a thick fog. Emily glanced at him, her stomach in knots. She had seen him at his most vulnerable—she had watched as he bled, as the fear for her had nearly broken him. But there was something else in his eyes now, something she couldn't quite place. A realization.

"You don't have to do this, Emily," Lucas said suddenly, his voice quiet but steady. He turned to her, his eyes locking with hers, and in that moment, she saw the pain, the guilt, and the love all coiled into one. "You don't have to stay. You can leave. I'll make sure you're safe."

The offer was genuine, but it broke her heart. He was trying to protect her, trying to push her away for her own good. He was willing to carry the burden alone if it meant she could escape.

The Cost

But she couldn't leave him. She wouldn't.

"I'm not going anywhere, Lucas," she said, her voice strong despite the uncertainty that gnawed at her. "I'm with you. We're in this together, no matter what."

He didn't answer right away, but she saw the tension in his shoulders ease just slightly. It wasn't much, but it was something. And that small gesture was enough to let her know that he understood. He didn't want her to get caught up in his mess, but in that moment, their fates were irrevocably linked.

They both stepped out of the car, their movements quiet but urgent. The house loomed in front of them, its shadow stretching out like a giant hand reaching toward them. The air felt heavy, thick with the promise of danger, but Emily didn't hesitate. She moved forward, her hand brushing against Lucas's as they approached the door. The sound of their footsteps was muffled by the rain, but it felt like the world was holding its breath.

The door creaked open as Lucas carefully unlocked it, the sound loud in the stillness of the night. They stepped inside, the musty scent of old wood and dust overwhelming at first. The house was abandoned, empty, save for the few pieces of furniture left behind, remnants of another time. It was exactly what they needed—a place to lay low, a place to breathe, even if only for a moment.

But as they stepped farther into the house, a cold chill swept over Emily. The feeling in her gut—one she had been ignoring for hours—was now undeniable. Something wasn't right. They weren't alone.

The hairs on the back of her neck stood up as she turned to Lucas, her eyes wide with realization. "Lucas... someone's been here."

He froze, his gaze darting around the darkened room. His hand instinctively went to the gun at his side, his posture alert, every muscle coiled in readiness. They weren't safe here, not anymore.

And then, from the corner of the room, a sound. A creak.

A whisper of movement.

Before either of them could react, a figure stepped out from the shadows, his face obscured by the dim light. The figure was tall, broad-shouldered, and moved with a quiet confidence that made every alarm in Emily's head scream.

"Did you think you could hide from us forever, Lucas?" the man said, his voice cold and mocking, the words hanging in the air like a death sentence.

Emily's heart sank as she recognized the man standing in front of them. He was one of them. One of the men who had been after Lucas for so long. And now, they were trapped again.

The cost of love, of standing by Lucas, had just become painfully clear. There was no escaping this. No way out.

The Cost

They had fallen too far. And the people hunting them were ready to finish what they had started.

In that moment, Emily knew there would be no easy way to win this fight. They had already lost so much, and now, the price of their love was becoming something far more dangerous than either of them had ever imagined.

Eleven

Divided

⁂

The world had shrunk into a narrow tunnel, and Emily could barely breathe. The figure standing in the dim light, just a few steps away, was all too familiar. The man who had cornered them, the one with the cold eyes and the icy grin, was one of the very people Lucas had feared. His presence filled the room like a storm about to break, and Emily's heart raced as she stood frozen, unsure of what to do.

Lucas moved slightly in front of her, his body a shield, though Emily knew it would take more than just a man standing in her way to keep them safe. They were trapped now—caught between a man who knew far too much and a storm that was only gathering strength. The darkness in the room seemed to grow deeper, more suffocating, and she could hear her breath, shallow and quick, as though her lungs could barely keep up with the tension.

Divided

The man's smirk didn't waver as he sized them up. His posture was casual, but the predatory glint in his eyes told a different story. He was enjoying this, savoring the moment, watching them squirm under the weight of their own fear.

"Well, well, well," the man said, his voice smooth, every word measured. "Lucas Gray. Thought you could outrun your past forever, huh?" He stepped forward, his boots barely making a sound against the creaky floorboards. "Did you really think you could disappear into the shadows of this city, live out your little happy ending? Did you honestly believe I'd just let you go?"

Lucas's eyes narrowed, his jaw tightening, but he didn't speak. Emily could feel the tension rising in his body like a coiled spring, but there was something else there—something deeper. The last few months had broken him in ways she hadn't fully understood. The weight of his family's legacy, of the people who had tormented him for years, had worn him down. And now, they were here. They had come for him. For both of them.

"I didn't run from anything," Lucas finally said, his voice low, almost calm. "I've been trying to stop you from coming after me. But you just won't stop, will you?"

The man laughed—a hollow, humorless sound. "You're a stubborn bastard, aren't you? I've been patient. Very patient. But all good things come to an end." He paused, letting the words sink in. "Your father built something great, Lucas. He had vision. He had power. And you? You've squandered it all. You've hidden in the shadows while the rest of us built empires."

Emily felt a pang of disgust at the way he spoke of Lucas's father. She could hear the reverence in his voice, but it wasn't respect. It was the kind of admiration you reserved for a king or a god—someone who controlled everything around them with an iron fist. The kind of man who would destroy anyone who stood in his way. And it had all been passed down to Lucas, like a dark inheritance.

"I didn't want any part of it," Lucas said, his voice barely above a whisper, yet the intensity in his words made Emily's chest tighten. "I wanted out. I wanted a life that wasn't defined by his legacy."

The man's smile faded slightly, replaced by a look of mock sympathy. "You think you could just walk away from all of this? From the power, from the connections? From the bloodshed? You think you can erase it just because you want to? It's too late for that. You can't just wash your hands of it, Lucas. You're in this whether you like it or not."

The words hit like a slap to the face. Emily could feel Lucas stiffen, the weight of everything he had tried to escape suddenly crashing back onto him. It wasn't just his family that had been chasing him—it was the entire world he had once been a part of, a world that wouldn't let him go.

And now, she was a part of it too.

A part of the mess, the danger, the lies.

Emily took a step closer to Lucas, her heart hammering in her chest. She wasn't going to stand back and watch him fall into the hands of these people. Not after everything they had been through. She wasn't going to let them take him away.

"I won't let you take him," she said, her voice steady despite the fear that coiled in her stomach. "You think you can just walk in here and take what you want? No. You're not getting away with it."

The man's gaze flickered to her, and for a moment, she saw the briefest flash of surprise in his eyes. Then, it was gone, replaced by a look of disdain.

"You really think you can stop this?" he asked, his voice dripping with contempt. "You're nothing more than a distraction. A temporary... comfort. You have no idea what you're dealing with."

Emily's breath caught in her throat. She knew what he was implying. He saw her as nothing more than a pawn in their game, a meaningless detail to be cast aside. But she wasn't going to let him win. She wasn't going to let anyone decide what her worth was.

"I'm not going anywhere," she said, her voice firm, unwavering. "And neither is he."

The man chuckled darkly, his hand reaching into his coat. Emily's eyes widened in panic as he pulled out a small, silenced handgun, the barrel glinting in the dim light. She could feel the room shift, the air growing heavy with impending violence.

Lucas reacted instinctively, his hand shooting out to grab her wrist and pull her back. "Stay behind me," he warned, his voice sharp. But there was no fear in his eyes—only a quiet resolve. He wasn't going to let her get hurt. Not now. Not ever.

The man took a step closer, the gun trained on Lucas. "You really think you can win this fight? You're weak, Lucas. You've always been weak. You ran from your father's empire, but in the end, you're nothing without it."

A fire lit in Lucas's eyes, a cold rage that Emily had never seen before. "You don't get it," he spat. "You think I'm weak because I didn't want any part of this. You think I'm weak because I didn't want to destroy everything in my path to get what I want. But the truth is, you're the weak one. You're the one who's been living in his shadow, waiting for him to give you what you think you deserve. And now, you're just a puppet."

The man's face twisted in fury at the insult, but before he could react, Lucas moved. Faster than Emily could blink, he lunged forward, his body colliding with the man's, sending him crashing into the wall. The gun flew from his hand, skittering across the floor.

Everything happened in a blur. Lucas and the man struggled, rolling across the room in a tangle of limbs, each trying to gain the upper hand. Emily moved without thinking, her hand grabbing the nearest object she could find—an old metal lamp—and raising it above her head. Without hesitation, she swung it at the man, the force of the blow knocking him back, stunning him for just a second.

Divided

Lucas took advantage of the momentary distraction, flipping the man onto his back and pinning him to the ground. His eyes locked with Emily's, and in that brief instant, she saw something she had never expected to see in him—vulnerability. But it was quickly replaced by determination.

"Go," he said, his voice low but urgent. "Get to the car. Now."

Emily hesitated, her heart in her throat. "I'm not leaving you."

"I'm not asking," he snapped, his grip tightening as he held the man down. "Go. Now."

Her pulse raced, but she didn't argue. She turned and ran, her feet pounding against the floor as she headed toward the door. The world outside felt like a different place, a place she had once known, a place that now seemed so distant and foreign. She could hear the sounds of the struggle behind her, the grunts, the shouts, the scuffle of shoes against wood.

But she didn't look back. She couldn't. Not when she knew what was at stake.

The cost of their love was too high, and they both knew it. This fight, this war, would change them forever. But Emily wasn't ready to give up—not now, not when they were so close. Not when she knew that as long as they had each other, they had a chance.

And that, at least, was worth fighting for.

Twelve

Test of Fate

The night was still dark when Emily reached the car, her breath coming in sharp gasps as she fumbled for the keys in her pocket. The distant sounds of footsteps echoed through the alleyway behind her, the heavy footsteps of men who had come for them. The car was just ahead—an old, nondescript sedan, its black paint reflecting the dull gleam of streetlights. But to her, it felt like the only thing standing between her and the chaos behind her. The one thing that could still give her and Lucas a fighting chance.

Her heart was in her throat, her hands shaking as she slid into the driver's seat and slammed the door shut. The car felt too small, too tight, like it was swallowing her whole. She wasn't sure how long she had before the men found them, before they realized Lucas was still inside the house. Before everything came crashing down.

Test of Fate

The engine roared to life as she turned the key in the ignition, and for a moment, it felt like time stopped. The world outside the car was a blur of shadow and rain, the lights of the city too far to reach. But Emily didn't look at the city. She didn't look at the road ahead. All she could see was the look in Lucas's eyes when he had told her to leave—to run while he fought the men who had come for them.

She hadn't left. She couldn't.

She stepped on the gas, pushing the car forward into the night, her fingers gripped tight around the steering wheel. There was a sound, faint at first, but unmistakable—the sound of a car engine roaring to life behind her. They weren't alone.

Emily's pulse quickened as she glanced in the rearview mirror. A set of headlights blinked on, growing brighter as the car behind them closed in. They were being followed. The realization hit her like a jolt of electricity, her breath catching in her chest.

She couldn't outrun them. They knew where they were going.

And yet, she couldn't stop. Not now.

Lucas's words echoed in her mind. "They won't stop until they have us. They're watching. Always watching." She had always known that the danger wasn't just a one-time thing, that it wouldn't go away once they found safety. But to be followed now, in the dead of night, with the weight of everything hanging in the balance—she wasn't sure how much longer they could keep running.

The car behind them was gaining speed, closing the distance with each passing second. Emily's grip tightened on the wheel. She had to think. She couldn't let them catch them. Not without a fight.

Without thinking, she swerved the car sharply to the left, into an alley that sliced between two tall buildings. Her tires screeched in protest as she accelerated, taking the corner too fast, but she didn't care. She couldn't afford to think about the consequences. They were both running on borrowed time now.

Behind her, the other car followed, the sound of its engine like thunder in the night. Emily glanced back through the rearview mirror again, her heart pounding harder as she saw the lights grow larger. They were closing in, and she couldn't outrun them for long.

She had to do something.

A plan, any plan, was better than waiting for them to catch up.

Ahead of her, the alley split in two—one path leading left toward a dead end, the other curving right toward a wider street. Emily made a snap decision, slamming the steering wheel to the right as the car fishtailed slightly, skidding into the second alley. She could hear the other car's tires squeal as they followed her, the sound growing closer, the engine roaring louder. But she wouldn't give them the satisfaction of thinking she was trapped. She wasn't done yet.

As they sped into the new alley, Emily spotted an open manhole cover ahead. It was risky, but she had no other choice. She took a deep breath and swerved the car to the right again, aiming for the small, narrow path between two buildings that led to the manhole. She could barely see the hole in the road, the darkness swallowing everything ahead of her. But she had faith in her instincts. She had to.

The car's tires hit the edge of the manhole, and for a split second, Emily felt the entire vehicle lift off the ground. Her stomach dropped, and the world spun wildly, but the car landed hard on the other side, its suspension absorbing the shock. Emily barely had time to react as she slammed the brakes to keep the car steady.

But when she looked back, her heart dropped.

The car behind them hadn't been as lucky.

It had driven straight into the open manhole, the tires spinning helplessly before the car lurched forward and crashed into the side of the street. The screeching of metal on concrete sent a shiver down her spine. She had done it. For now, at least, they were safe. But she knew better than to think this was over.

She turned back to Lucas, who had remained silent the entire time, his body tense beside her. The darkness in his eyes seemed to deepen as he met her gaze, and for a brief moment, she saw something in him that she hadn't noticed before—a weariness, an acceptance. They had survived the night, but they both knew they couldn't keep running forever.

"Lucas, we're not out of this yet," Emily said, her voice breaking the silence, but the fear in it was undeniable. "We can't outrun them. We need a plan."

He nodded slowly, his eyes still fixed on the road ahead, the weight of everything they had gone through pressing down on his shoulders. "I know," he muttered. "We need to go somewhere they'll never find us."

Emily swallowed hard, the plan that had started to form in her mind solidifying into something both terrifying and necessary. She didn't know how much more of this she could take, how much more of the constant fear, the never-ending chase. But she knew there was no turning back. The man who had almost taken Lucas's life—who had tried to destroy everything they had—wasn't the end. He was just one piece of the puzzle.

Lucas's eyes flickered to hers, his expression hardened. "There's one place I know we can go. It's off the grid. No one will know where we are."

Emily nodded. "Where?"

He hesitated, his hand tightening around the passenger seat as if he was unsure whether he should tell her. Finally, he spoke, his voice low. "It's an old hideout. My father's. A place he used for meetings, for… other things. It's been abandoned for years. No one knows about it."

Emily's heart skipped a beat. The thought of going into one of the last places connected to Lucas's father's empire sent a chill down her spine. But the thought of being cornered—of being hunted—was even worse.

"Are you sure?" she asked, her voice quiet, but filled with an edge of fear. "It could be dangerous."

"Everything's dangerous now," Lucas replied, his gaze hardening. "But it's the only place left. We have no choice."

Emily's mind raced. This was it—the crossroads they had been heading toward. The final decision. There would be no more running. No more hiding. The man who had chased them tonight, and all the others connected to him, would be there, waiting for them. But if they didn't face this head-on, if they didn't take the chance, they would never have a future. They would never have peace.

She nodded, her jaw setting with resolve. "Let's go."

Lucas didn't say anything more. He didn't need to. They both knew what was at stake. What they would be risking.

And as they drove through the night, leaving the wreckage of their past behind, Emily couldn't shake the feeling that this was their last chance. The last opportunity to walk away from this war, to walk away with their lives.

But as they drove deeper into the night, toward the place where it had all begun, she couldn't escape the feeling that the real battle— the one that would truly test them—was just beginning.

Thirteen

Universes

The car seemed to hum with an ominous energy as it sped through the night. The streetlights outside flickered weakly as they passed, their glow barely piercing the thick darkness. Lucas drove with a steady hand, his face tight with determination, but his eyes, sharp and alert, never stopped scanning the road ahead. The weight of the night was heavy, pressing down on him like the cold grip of a hand that refused to let go.

Emily sat beside him, the silence between them oppressive. She could feel the tension in the air, the feeling that something was about to break, but she couldn't place what it was. It was more than the danger. More than the men who had been hunting them for so long. There was something bigger, something darker at play, and it felt as if the universe itself was on the verge of collapsing around them.

As the car bounced over the uneven road, Emily glanced at Lucas. His jaw was clenched, his brow furrowed as if he was in the midst of some internal struggle. She wanted to say something, to reach out to him, but she didn't know how. The truth was, she wasn't sure what to say anymore. They had crossed too many lines. They had gotten too far into this world of danger and violence to pretend like everything could go back to normal. They couldn't go back.

"Lucas," she said softly, breaking the silence, her voice shaking with a mix of fear and resolve. "What if this is the end? What if we don't make it out of this? I mean, what happens then?"

Lucas's grip on the steering wheel tightened. He didn't answer right away, his gaze fixed on the road ahead, as if the question hadn't reached him yet. But then, he glanced at her, his eyes dark and filled with something she couldn't decipher.

"Then we face it together," he said, his voice low, almost a whisper. "We've made it this far. That means something."

Emily's heart thudded in her chest, but the weight of his words was like a chain around her lungs. She wanted to believe him. She wanted to believe that no matter what happened, no matter how deep into the darkness they fell, they would come out on the other side. But the fear that had been gnawing at her from the inside was still there, growing, feeding on her doubts.

They weren't just running from the men who had found them. They were running from an entire world—an empire—that Lucas's father had built, one that still stretched out in every direction, a web of power and corruption that refused to let go. But it was more than that. This was about their love—about how they had found each other in the wreckage of their lives, only to be torn apart by the very forces that had shaped them.

The world was collapsing around them. Their worlds.

The safe house was just up ahead—a crumbling mansion on the outskirts of the city, hidden away in a forgotten corner of the world. It had once been a place of power, a place where deals were made, secrets were traded, and lives were shattered in the pursuit of something greater. And now, it was their last chance. The only place left where they could hide.

As Lucas turned the car onto the long, winding driveway that led to the mansion, Emily felt her chest tighten. The house loomed ahead, an ancient, decaying structure that had been abandoned for years. The windows were dark, the once-grand exterior now covered in ivy and dirt. But to Lucas, it was still home. Still a place where he could regroup. Where he could make his stand.

He pulled the car to a stop in front of the massive, wooden doors, the engine idling as the sound of the rain beating against the roof filled the silence. Emily didn't move. She just stared at the mansion in front of them, her mind racing with every possibility. Every outcome. What would happen when they went inside? Would they be safe? Or was this just another trap? Another false promise of safety that would fall apart the moment they stepped through the door?

But there was no time for second-guessing. They couldn't afford to doubt themselves now.

"Are you ready for this?" Lucas asked, his voice barely audible above the sound of the rain. He turned to look at her, his eyes searching her face for something he needed—something he had been waiting for. And in that moment, Emily saw the depth of his desperation, the weight of everything he had carried with him for so long.

"No," Emily whispered, her voice barely a breath. "But I'm ready to try."

She stepped out of the car, the cold air immediately hitting her skin as she made her way toward the front door. Lucas followed closely behind, his hand hovering at his side, where his gun rested. They weren't going to make it through this without a fight. They both knew that.

The door creaked open with a heavy groan as Lucas pushed it forward, revealing the dark interior of the mansion. The air inside smelled of dust and decay, the remnants of a life long gone. The hallway stretched out in front of them, dimly lit by the flickering lights overhead, casting long shadows across the worn marble floors.

Lucas didn't hesitate. He moved forward, his footsteps echoing through the silence, as if the house itself was holding its breath. Emily followed him, her heart pounding in her chest, her senses alert to every sound, every movement.

They moved through the house quickly, making their way to the back, where the hidden room was. It had been his father's private office, the place where the real deals were made, the place where the empire had been built. And it was where Lucas had hidden the key to everything—the plans, the documents, the connections that could bring down everything his father had created.

But as they turned the corner into the back hallway, something felt wrong. The air was still. The silence was too thick. Emily's breath caught in her throat as her eyes flicked to the side, to the shadowy corner of the room. And then she saw it.

The door was ajar.

It hadn't been opened in years. No one had come in here. No one except them.

She froze, every instinct in her body screaming at her to turn and run. But she couldn't. Not now. Not when they had come this far.

Lucas noticed her hesitation, and his body tensed beside her. "Stay close," he whispered, his voice barely audible. He moved toward the door slowly, his eyes scanning the room for any sign of movement.

Emily followed, her heart in her throat. She couldn't shake the feeling that they had walked into a trap. It wasn't just about Lucas's enemies anymore. It was about the things that were still hidden in the dark corners of this house—secrets, lies, and old ghosts that had never truly gone away.

As they reached the door, Lucas pushed it open gently, his gun raised. The room beyond was just as she had imagined—dark, quiet, and full of the weight of years of history. The desk sat against the far wall, papers strewn across it in chaotic disarray. The walls were lined with bookshelves, filled with old leather-bound volumes that looked like they had never been touched.

But there was something else in the room, something that caught Emily's attention before she could even comprehend what she was seeing.

The files on the desk were open, half-sorted, and covered with a thin layer of dust. But they weren't the papers Lucas had left behind. They were new. Recent. And they had her name on them.

Her heart skipped a beat.

"Lucas," she whispered, her voice trembling as she stepped forward, reaching for the papers. "These aren't from your father."

Lucas's eyes snapped to hers, his expression darkening as he saw the papers in her hands. The words written on them, the files marked with her name, the very thing she had feared the most: They had been watching her all along.

"We were never meant to escape," Lucas said, his voice quiet, cold. "This was always going to happen. They've been planning this from the beginning."

The room felt like it was closing in around them, the weight of everything bearing down on them with the force of a collapsing star. All of their actions, all their choices, had led them here—into the center of the storm. And the worst part was, there was no way out.

Emily looked at Lucas, her heart breaking as she realized the truth of what he had said. Their world was already falling apart. The enemies they had tried to outrun, the world they had tried to escape, had already claimed them. And no matter how much they fought, no matter how much they ran, the universe had already decided their fate.

Their worlds—his and hers—had collided. And the impact was far worse than either of them could have ever imagined.

There was no escaping what had been set in motion. There was no undoing the damage. The cost of love had already been paid in full. And now, as the walls of their lives crumbled around them, Emily and Lucas were left with nothing but the ruins of their choices.

And the final test of fate awaited them.

Fourteen

Love in the Void

T he mansion felt suffocating now. The air seemed thick with the weight of every secret, every betrayal that had ever taken place within these walls. Emily stood motionless, holding the files in her hands, the weight of what they meant pressing down on her chest like an unrelenting force. The papers, the names, the connections—they were all pointing toward her. Toward them. Toward everything she had fought to protect.

Lucas stood beside her, his eyes narrowing as he scanned the documents. His face, once so composed, was now etched with the rawness of the reality they were facing. He had known the danger was always there, lurking in the shadows, but this—this was a confirmation of everything he had feared. The world he had tried to leave behind, the empire his father had built, was not going to let him go. And neither was Emily. Neither was the life they had tried to carve out for themselves.

His hands clenched into fists at his sides as he looked at the papers. "They've been planning this all along," he muttered, his voice barely a whisper. "You were never meant to be free. They knew we'd come here."

Emily felt the coldness of his words settle in her bones. It wasn't just about Lucas anymore. It wasn't just about the men who had hunted him, or the legacy of his father that had haunted him for so long. It was about them—about their lives, about everything they had built together, about the love they had shared.

"They've been watching us," she said, her voice trembling as she looked at him. "From the very beginning. They knew about us, Lucas. They knew everything. And they used me. They used us."

Lucas turned away, running a hand through his hair, his frustration palpable. "They always knew. I thought I could protect you, Emily. I thought I could keep you out of this. But I was wrong. I can't protect you from this. I can't protect either of us anymore."

Emily's heart clenched as she looked at him, the pain in his eyes mirroring her own. She had been so focused on the danger, on the chase, on the escape that she hadn't fully realized the gravity of their situation. The deeper they had gotten into this world, the more they had become entangled in the web of deceit, manipulation, and power. And now, there was no way out.

"We're not alone in this," she said, her voice steady now, though the weight of the truth was suffocating. "There's a whole network. This isn't just about your father. It's bigger than that. It's a system. And they're not just going to stop coming for us."

Lucas's gaze flicked to her, his eyes darkening. "I know. But what do we do now, Emily? What's left for us?"

Emily felt a chill run down her spine at the question. What was left? Was there anything left for them? Was there any way to undo the damage that had already been done? Her mind raced, searching for an answer, any answer. But the truth was, she didn't have one. All she knew was that they couldn't keep running forever. The world they were fighting against was too big, too powerful, and they were just two people trying to survive in a world that was already broken.

She glanced at the room around them—the mansion that had once held so much power, so much potential—and for the first time, she saw it for what it truly was: a trap. It wasn't just a place to hide. It was a cage.

"We can't stay here," Emily said, her voice resolute. "They'll come for us here. They'll find us, just like they found us before."

Lucas's jaw tightened, but he didn't argue. He knew she was right. He had known it all along. They had used this house as a place to regroup, to catch their breath, but it wasn't safe. It never had been. And now, it felt like the walls were closing in.

"We need to move," Lucas said, his voice hardening with determination. "But where do we go? Where can we hide?"

Emily didn't have an answer, not a clear one. But one thing was certain—if they stayed here, they wouldn't survive. They would be found. They would be caught. The men who were after them, the network that had been tracking them, would never stop until they had destroyed everything. They had to find a way to fight back. They had to find a way to escape.

A plan, any plan, was better than waiting for the inevitable.

As the seconds ticked by, the pressure of their situation seemed to grow heavier, suffocating them both. Emily felt trapped—not just by the walls of the mansion, but by the weight of everything they had lost. The choices they had made. The things they had sacrificed. And yet, despite the darkness that had closed in around them, despite the fear that threatened to consume her, she knew that they had one thing left.

Each other.

In this broken world, the only thing that still mattered—the only thing that could save them—was the love they shared. But even that, she knew, came with a price.

She turned to Lucas, meeting his gaze. "We fight. We fight back. We take everything they've built and tear it down. Together."

Lucas's eyes softened, the hardness in his features melting away, replaced by a flicker of something she hadn't seen in him for a long time: hope. It was small, fleeting, but it was enough.

"Together," he repeated, his voice barely above a whisper.

But even as he spoke, Emily could feel the weight of their choices pressing down on them. It was one thing to say they would fight back. It was another thing entirely to take on the empire that had controlled their lives, controlled everything, for so long.

The sound of footsteps echoed in the hallway outside the room, snapping Emily and Lucas out of their shared moment. The danger was real. The fight wasn't just hypothetical anymore. It was here. They didn't have time for plans or strategies. They had to act.

"We don't have time," Emily said, her voice urgent. "We need to go. Now."

Lucas didn't hesitate. He moved quickly toward the door, his hand on the handle, his eyes scanning the room one last time. But Emily didn't follow him immediately. She stayed where she was for a moment, staring at the papers on the desk—the ones with her name on them, the ones that had led them here.

This was no longer just about surviving. It was about fighting for the life they had dreamed of—the life they had lost somewhere along the way. She wasn't going to let that slip away. Not without a fight.

With a final glance at Lucas, she grabbed the papers from the desk and shoved them into her bag. She wasn't going to let them take everything from her. Not now.

She joined him at the door, her heart pounding in her chest, and together, they stepped into the unknown. The mansion's shadows stretched long and dark in front of them, and behind them, the sound of their pursuers grew louder.

But they were no longer running from the past. They weren't hiding anymore. This was their fight, and they would face it, no matter the cost.

The world might have been collapsing, but for the first time in a long while, Emily felt like she had a chance. A chance to rewrite the end of their story. A chance to fight back.

And this time, there was no turning back.

Not for either of them.

Fifteen

Rebond

The sound of their footsteps was the only thing that cut through the stillness of the mansion as Lucas and Emily moved swiftly, yet cautiously, through the dimly lit hallways. Every shadow seemed to stretch longer than the last, the old walls creaking and groaning under the weight of their presence as if the house was awake and watching them. Emily's heartbeat in her throat, each thudding pulse a reminder that their time was running out. Their only chance for survival was to escape. To get out of this place before their enemies found them.

But the longer they stayed, the more Emily felt the mansion's walls close in around them. It wasn't just the physical space. It was the weight of everything they had fought against, the weight of everything that had led them here. The choices, the mistakes, the pieces of their lives shattered beyond recognition. They couldn't outrun their pasts forever. The empire Lucas's father had built was like a shadow that would never let them go, no matter how far they ran.

"Stay close," Lucas murmured, his voice tight as he led her down another hallway, his hand hovering at his side where the gun rested. The uncertainty in his voice wasn't lost on her. For the first time since they had entered the mansion, Emily felt the raw vulnerability of their situation. This wasn't just about fighting for their survival anymore. This was about the war they were waging against a world that had already claimed their fates.

Emily didn't speak. She just nodded, her breath shallow and quick as she kept her pace behind him. She could hear the sound of approaching footsteps from the hallway ahead, and her stomach dropped. They weren't alone anymore. Someone else had come for them.

"Lucas," she whispered urgently, her eyes darting toward the door at the far end of the hallway. "We're running out of time."

He stopped, turning to look at her with a fierce intensity in his eyes. "We make time," he said, his voice filled with quiet determination. "We make our own choices now."

Emily felt a wave of cold wash over her at the finality in his words. This wasn't just about survival anymore. It was about taking control. Taking back what they had lost. But even as the thought settled in her mind, she couldn't shake the feeling that they were being herded into a trap. Every step they took felt like a step closer to something they couldn't escape.

Suddenly, the sound of a door creaking open echoed down the hallway. A figure appeared at the end of the hall, a silhouette in the dim light. Emily's breath caught in her throat. It was one of them. One of the men who had been hunting them.

"Lucas," she breathed, fear creeping into her voice. "It's him.

It's him!"

Lucas's eyes locked onto hers, and in that moment, she saw it—the same fear, the same desperation that had been buried deep inside him for so long. They had both known it was coming, but now that it was here, the reality of their situation hit with a crushing weight.

Without a word, Lucas stepped in front of her, his body a shield, as he aimed the gun at the approaching figure. The man's face remained obscured by the shadows, but Emily could feel the tension in the air as he moved closer.

"Get back," Lucas said, his voice steady but filled with a quiet urgency. "Don't move."

But Emily didn't listen. Her instincts told her that now was not the time to stay hidden. She needed to act. She had to fight back. She couldn't stand by while the man who had caused them so much pain took control of their fate.

She moved before Lucas could stop her, her hand reaching for the knife she had tucked into her waistband. The weight of the blade was familiar now, a reminder of the choices they had made to survive. She wouldn't let anyone take him from her. Not now.

"Lucas, move!" Emily shouted as she lunged toward the man, her heart pounding in her ears. The knife glinted in the dim light as she aimed for the man's side.

The man reacted quickly, sidestepping her attempt to strike, his hand grabbing her wrist and twisting it with a force that sent pain shooting up her arm. She gasped, but before she could recover, he pushed her back against the wall, the force of the impact knocking the breath from her lungs.

"Emily!" Lucas shouted, but his voice was barely audible above the rush of blood in her ears.

The man turned his attention to Lucas, a wicked smile twisting his lips. He was tall, muscular, and his face was cold, devoid of any emotion. He didn't need to say anything for Emily to know who he was. He was the one who had been chasing them—the one who had orchestrated everything.

Lucas moved quickly, his body twisting as he brought the gun up, aiming at the man. But before he could fire, the man lunged at him, knocking the gun from his hands and sending him sprawling onto the floor.

The world seemed to slow as Emily watched in horror, her pulse racing. She couldn't lose him. She couldn't lose him now.

"Lucas!" she screamed, scrambling to her feet, her heart pounding in her chest.

The man turned toward her, his eyes locking onto hers, and for a moment, Emily saw something in his gaze—something that made her stomach turn. This wasn't just about Lucas anymore. This was about something bigger. Something more dangerous than she had ever imagined.

"You're too late," the man sneered, his voice low and menacing. "You've already lost."

Emily's heart pounded in her chest as she saw the man raise his fist, preparing to strike. But she couldn't let him. Not now. Not when everything was on the line.

Her instincts kicked in. She moved before she thought, rushing toward the man with the blade in her hand. She didn't hesitate. She didn't think about the consequences. She just acted.

The man turned just in time to catch the edge of the blade across his arm. He grunted, staggering back, but his eyes flashed with fury. With a roar, he lunged toward her, his hands gripping her throat in a vice-like grip.

Emily gasped for air, her vision blurring as his grip tightened, cutting off her breath. She struggled, her hands clawing at his, but his strength was overwhelming. Her body went limp, her lungs screaming for air, but it felt like everything was slipping away.

"Emily!" Lucas shouted, his voice barely audible above the ringing in her ears.

Just as Emily thought she couldn't fight any longer, a gunshot rang out. The man's grip loosened, and he staggered backward, his eyes wide with disbelief. He fell to the floor with a heavy thud, blood spilling from the wound in his chest.

Emily gasped, sucking in a deep breath as she collapsed to her knees, her hands shaking. She looked up to see Lucas standing there, his gun in his hand, his face grim.

"Are you okay?" he asked, his voice rough but filled with concern as he knelt beside her.

Emily could barely speak. She nodded, her breath ragged as she tried to steady herself. The pain in her chest from his grip was still there, a reminder of how close she had come to losing everything.

"We can't stay here," Lucas said, his voice filled with urgency. "There's more coming. We need to move. Now."

Emily stood shakily, still reeling from the adrenaline, but she didn't hesitate. They had come this far. They had survived this fight. But she knew this wasn't the end. It couldn't be.

She grabbed his hand, and together, they moved through the mansion, the weight of everything they had lost, everything they had fought for, pressing down on them like a storm they couldn't outrun.

The fight wasn't over. Not by a long shot.

And as they fled into the night, Emily knew one thing for

certain: there was no turning back. There was only forward—through the darkness, through the void—fighting for a future they weren't sure they would ever see. But it was the only choice they had left.

And together, they would face it.

www.ingramcontent.com/pod-product-compliance
Lightning Source LLC
LaVergne TN
LVHW010550070526
838199LV00063BA/4926